EFFECTS OF SEXUAL ASSAULT AND SEXUAL HARASSMENT ON SEPARATION FROM THE U.S. MILITARY

Findings from the 2014 RAND Military Workplace Study

Andrew R. Morral, Miriam Matthews, Matthew Cefalu,
Terry L. Schell, Linda Cottrell

Prepared for the Office of the Secretary of Defense
Approved for public release; distribution unlimited

For more information on this publication, visit www.rand.org/t/RR870z10

Library of Congress Cataloging-in-Publication Data is available for this publication.
ISBN: 978-1-9774-0655-2

Published by the RAND Corporation, Santa Monica, Calif.
© Copyright 2021 RAND Corporation
RAND® is a registered trademark.

Support RAND
Make a tax-deductible charitable contribution at
www.rand.org/giving/contribute

www.rand.org

Preface

The U.S. Department of Defense (DoD) Sexual Assault Prevention and Response Office contracted with the RAND Corporation to provide a new and independent evaluation of sexual assault, sexual harassment, and gender discrimination across the U.S. military. DoD asked the RAND research team to assess and, if necessary, redesign the approach used in previous DoD surveys, if such changes would improve the accuracy and validity of the survey results for estimating the prevalence of sexual crimes and other violations of military law. RAND found that some of DoD's survey methodology was in keeping with industry best practices. However, RAND recommended changes to DoD's sexual assault and sexual harassment metrics to be more in line with language used in military law and policy. In the summer of 2014, RAND fielded these updated measures in a new survey as part of the RAND Military Workplace Study.

This report describes data analyses designed to assess the effects, if any, of experiences of sexual assault, sexual harassment, or both on service members' decisions to separate from the military. The complete series that collectively describes the study methodology and its findings, to date, includes the following reports, in order of when they were produced:

- *Sexual Assault and Sexual Harassment in the U.S. Military: Top-Line Estimates for Active-Duty Service Members from the 2014 RAND Military Workplace Study*
- *Sexual Assault and Sexual Harassment in the U.S. Military: Top-Line Estimates for Active-Duty Coast Guard Members from the 2014 RAND Military Workplace Study*
- *Sexual Assault and Sexual Harassment in the U.S. Military: Volume 1. Design of the 2014 RAND Military Workplace Study*
- *Sexual Assault and Sexual Harassment in the U.S. Military: Volume 2. Estimates for Department of Defense Service Members from the 2014 RAND Military Workplace Study*
- *Sexual Assault and Sexual Harassment in the U.S. Military: Annex to Volume 2. Tabular Results from the 2014 RAND Military Workplace Study for Department of Defense Service Members*
- *Sexual Assault and Sexual Harassment in the U.S. Military: Volume 3. Estimates for Coast Guard Service Members from the 2014 RAND Military Workplace Study*

- *Sexual Assault and Sexual Harassment in the U.S. Military: Annex to Volume 3. Tabular Results from the 2014 RAND Military Workplace Study for Coast Guard Service Members*
- *Sexual Assault and Sexual Harassment in the U.S. Military: Volume 4. Investigations of Potential Bias in Estimates from the 2014 RAND Military Workplace Study*
- *Sexual Assault and Sexual Harassment in the U.S. Military: Volume 5. Estimates for Installation- and Command-Level Risk of Sexual Assault and Sexual Harassment from the 2014 RAND Military Workplace Study*
- *Sexual Assault and Sexual Harassment in the U.S. Military: Annex to Volume 5. Tabular Results from the 2014 RAND Military Workplace Study for Installation- and Command-Level Risk of Sexual Assault and Sexual Harassment*
- *Risk Factors for Sexual Assault and Sexual Harassment in the U.S. Military: Findings from the 2014 RAND Military Workplace Study*
- *Effects of Sexual Assault and Sexual Harassment on Separation from the U.S. Military: Findings from the 2014 RAND Military Workplace Study.*

These reports are available online at www.rand.org/surveys/rmws.

The research reported here was completed in December 2018 and underwent security review with the sponsor and the Defense Office of Prepublication and Security Review before public release.

This research was sponsored by the U.S. Department of Defense and conducted within the Forces and Resources Policy Center of the RAND National Security Research Division (NSRD), which operates the National Defense Research Institute (NDRI), a federally funded research and development center sponsored by the Office of the Secretary of Defense, the Joint Staff, the Unified Combatant Commands, the Navy, the Marine Corps, the defense agencies, and the defense intelligence enterprise.

For more information on the Forces and Resources Policy Center, see www.rand.org/nsrd/frp or contact the director (contact information is provided on the webpage).

Contents

Figure and Tables

Figure

Tables

Summary

Sexual assault and sexual harassment can have harmful consequences for those who are targeted, including short- and long-term effects on psychological and physical health, associated and sometimes costly and time-consuming treatment needs, job dissatisfaction, and other hardships (Dichter and True, 2015; Fitzgerald, Drasgow, and Magley, 1999; Frayne et al., 1999; Turchik and Wilson, 2010; Willness, Steel, and Lee, 2007). In addition to having consequences that are largely borne by the target of the abuse, sexual assault and sexual harassment may have deleterious and costly consequences in general for employers if the abuse results in higher turnover or low morale and productivity.

In this report, we seek to quantify the effects of sexual assault and sexual harassment on separations from the U.S. military and, by extension, the effects on military costs and readiness; one way we do this is by considering the number of person-hours associated with separations that are earlier than would otherwise be expected.[1] Specifically, we examine all separations, whether these occurred because service members voluntarily chose not to re-enlist or continue their service as an officer or because they were discharged from the military for reasons other than their choice not to renew their commitment to serve. In addition, we examine the reasons recorded for these separations and whether the service members whose survey responses led us to classify them as having been sexually assaulted or sexually harassed were more likely to (1) leave the military of their own volition or (2) be discharged for reasons associated with their failure to meet expectations for their performance or conduct.

---

[1] In the results from the survey described in this report, reference to *sexual assault* is based on survey respondents' answers to questions about their experiences but does not reflect whether a sexual assault was substantiated by an investigation. In addition, reference to *sexual harassment* is also based on survey respondents' answers to questions about their experiences and does not reflect whether sexual harassment was substantiated by an investigation. Use of the terms *perpetrator* and *victim* in this report are not intended to presume the guilt or innocence of an individual.

Methods

To conduct these analyses, we drew on personnel records and the RAND Military Workplace Study (RMWS), a large-scale survey of sexual assault and sexual harassment experiences conducted in 2014 (see Morral, Gore, and Schell, 2014). Specifically, we analyzed separations from the military among a cohort of 145,300 RMWS active-component respondents during the 28 months after their inclusion in the RMWS sample frame. These respondents were weighted to be representative of the full 1,317,561 service members in the active component as of April 2014. Members of this cohort were counted as having separated from the military if, at any point during the 28-month observation period, they were no longer a member of either the active or reserve component of the U.S. military according to personnel records maintained by the Defense Manpower Data Center.

We used a logistic regression model to estimate the effects of sexual assault and sexual harassment on separations from the military. To ensure that we accurately captured any nonlinear effects of the covariates on separations, we first estimated a nonlinear, machine-learning model predicting separations in the full population of 1.3 million active-component members based on the following person-level characteristics:

- gender
- age
- race
- ethnicity
- educational level (six categories)
- marital status
- number of dependents
- service branch
- pay grade (seven levels)[2]
- location (state or country)
- occupational group (20 categories)
- months deployed in career
- months deployed in past 12 months
- date of commission or enlistment
- source of commission or enlistment
- active-duty end date[3]
- months of active-duty service (lifetime)

---

[2]   The seven pay grade levels were (1) E1–E3, (2) E4, (3), E5–E6, (4) E7–E9, (5) W1–W5, (6) O1–O3, and (7) O4–O6. The pay grades were grouped to facilitate interpretability of group comparisons.

[3]   The active-duty end date represents the conclusion of a commitment to active military service and is a point at which individuals may choose to separate from such service. All else being equal, those with an earlier active-duty end date might be expected to separate earlier than those with a later active-duty end date.

- Armed Forces Qualification Test score (enlisted only)
- strength accounting code
- time in current pay grade (normalized)
- time in previous pay grade (normalized).[4]

We now review additional information regarding how these characteristics were incorporated into the final model. Statistically significant bivariate results led us to incorporate the selected characteristics into analyses. Specifically, we included these characteristics in analyses to account for their possible associations with separation, either voluntary or involuntary, from the military. Inclusion of the characteristics allowed us to assess the effects of sexual assault and sexual harassment (both based on our classifications of individuals by survey responses) on separation above and beyond the effects of these characteristics.

As described in more detail in Chapter Two, we used generalized boosted regression (see Ridgeway, 2018) with four-way interactions to fit an adaptive, nonlinear regression of separations on the 21 variables listed earlier.[5] Optimal model complexity was assessed using fivefold cross-validation, and the final model selected was the iteration that minimized the cross-validated error of prediction. Models were fit using a logit link and loss function, and the predicted log odds of separation was the output for each individual. The log odds of separation were then incorporated in a standard general linear model (a logistic regression model), along with other covariates, to estimate the effect of sexual assault and sexual harassment on separation in the weighted sample of RMWS respondents.

The Effects of Sexual Assault and Sexual Harassment on Separation

We found that sexual assault and sexual harassment were uniquely associated with subsequent separation from the military—specifically, they increased the odds of separation (sexual assault odds ratio = 2.03, with a 95% confidence interval [CI]: 1.50–2.70; sexual harassment odds ratio = 1.70, with a 95% CI: 1.42–2.04). Overall, we estimate that 5,600 (95% CI: 4,600–7,000) of the 21,000 (95% CI: 19,100–23,000) service members estimated to have been sexually assaulted in fiscal year (FY) 2014 left the military in the subsequent 28-month period. Although some of these service members

---

[4]   For active-duty end date, strength accounting code, time in current pay grade, and time in previous pay grade, the values were determined as of September 2013, which was the beginning of the period over which past-year sexual assault and sexual harassment were assessed in the RMWS.

[5]   Generalized boosted regressions can be used for prediction from a large number of variables while also permitting flexible, nonlinear relationships between variables. They provide a more flexible approach to modeling than do parametric logistic regression models that assume that variables are linear and additive on the log-odds scale (McCaffrey, Ridgeway, and Morral, 2004).

would have left the military even if they had not been sexually assaulted, our analyses suggest that there were 2,000 (95% CI: 1,100–3,100) more separations than would be predicted had these individuals not been assaulted. In addition, we estimate that 28,200 (95% CI: 24,300–32,800) of 117,000 (95% CI: 110,500–123,500) service members estimated to have been sexually harassed in FY 2014 separated from the service over the 28-month period that we examined. Accounting for other service member characteristics that may be associated with separation, we estimate that there were approximately 8,000 (95% CI: 5,100–11,200) more separations of sexually harassed service members than would be predicted had these individuals not been harassed.[6]

It is worth noting that these are the separations during the observation period (essentially, FYs 2015–2016) that were associated with just the sexual assaults or sexual harassment occurring in FY 2014. These analyses account for sexual assaults or sexual harassment only during the observation period and cannot account for the associations between separation and experiences of sexual assault or harassment at points outside the observation period. There is an unknown number of additional separations during the observation period that were associated with sexual assaults or sexual harassment that occurred either before or after FY 2014. Thus, the percentage of all separations within the period that might be attributable to sexual assault or sexual harassment is likely to be considerably higher than the percentages presented here, which were restricted to events in a single year.

Higher separation rates among those who were sexually assaulted or sexually harassed could be voluntary or involuntary. That is, these members might have preferred to leave the service, or they might have been discharged by the military for cause, such as alcoholism, crime, insubordination, or failure to meet minimum requirements. We grouped such reasons into a category called *discharges for failure to adhere to standards or expectations.* Our results strongly suggest that separations following sexual assaults are more likely to be voluntary than involuntary for both men and women, and this tendency to leave voluntarily is even greater for men. Overall, this suggests that those who are sexually assaulted or sexually harassed are more likely to choose to separate than to be discharged for cause, which suggests that the experience of sexual assault or sexual harassment contributes to a desire to leave the military.

Not all service members report when they are sexually assaulted, but reporting makes a wide variety of services and response systems available to these members. At the same time, reporting has been associated with perceived social retaliation, which is one of the reasons service members give for choosing not to report a sexual assault (Morral, Gore, and Schell, 2015a). We examined whether those who self-reported filing an official report about the assault were more or less likely to separate over the observa-

---

[6] These estimates are for the full active-duty military population. The sample weights use the same types of weighting strategies that DoD uses to produce estimates about the full population when analyzing the Workplace and Gender Relations Survey of Active Duty Members, even though only a subset of the population takes the survey (for more information on weighting, see Morral, Gore, and Schell, 2014).

tion period, but we found no significant association between reporting and separation rates.[7] This analysis had low statistical power, so it had little chance of detecting an association, even if one exists.

Most sexual assaults of members in the military involve unwanted touching by a coworker, and some might count as instances of sexual harassment, such as if the unwanted behavior is pervasive or severe, creating a hostile work environment.[8] This raises the possibility that the association we found between sexual harassment and elevated separation rates merely reflects the fact that many who were sexually harassed were also assaulted, and those who were assaulted separate at higher rates. We ruled this possibility out, however, by showing that members who were sexually harassed but not sexually assaulted also had an elevated risk of separation. Indeed, the effect of sexual harassment was quite similar whether we included or excluded individuals who were also assaulted.

This observation highlights that sexual harassment itself is a serious threat to long-term readiness, independently of its frequent association with sexual assault. This is consistent with prior research (Murdoch et al., 2006), including research that has found that the experience of sexual harassment may undermine a service member's confidence that the military can provide a safe and supportive workplace (Schneider, Swan, and Fitzgerald, 1997). Whereas civilian employees are covered by Title VII of the Civil Rights Act of 1964 (Pub. L. 88-352) and can pursue legal action against their employers if the workplace is not safe from unlawful harassment (Fitzgerald, Swan, and Fischer, 1995; Sagawa and Campbell, 1992), Title VII does not apply to uniformed military personnel, so this response strategy is not available to active-duty service members (Sagawa and Campbell, 1992). Furthermore, service members, unlike civilian workers, are generally unable to switch to a new employer at a time of their choosing. However, victims may choose to avoid extending their current military commitment, thus affecting military retention.

In addition to the personal costs borne by service members classified as having experienced sexual assault or sexual harassment, the large number of separations associated with these forms of misconduct represent a significant cost to the U.S. military. Costs of personnel losses vary depending on the service member's service branch, years of service, and career specialty; whether the service is growing or shrinking; replacement recruiting costs and incentives; and many other factors. Moreover, although our analyses suggest that, over a 28-month period, 2,000 separations (95% CI: 1,100–3,100) were associated with sexual assault and 8,000 (95% CI: 5,100–11,200) were

---

[7] An official report regarding possible experiences of sexual assault could have been a restricted report, an unrestricted report, or both.

[8] Unwanted sexual touching that meets the definition of a sexual assault would generally count as severe. It need not be pervasive to qualify as sexual harassment. This unwanted touching can take place off duty and away from a military facility, and it would still count as sexual harassment if done by a coworker.

associated with sexual harassment, they do not indicate how much longer members would have served had they not been assaulted or harassed. Therefore, the exact costs of the personnel losses highlighted in our analyses are unclear. However, because the minimum re-enlistment period is typically two years, the services are losing a minimum of 16,000 manpower years prematurely, and probably much more than this, as a result of separations associated with sexual assault and sexual harassment. Furthermore, recruitment and training costs are being moved to an earlier time than would have been required had the services retained these individuals.

These findings suggest several steps that DoD, including each of the military services, could take to better address the costs to service members and DoD of sexual assault and sexual harassment. For instance, DoD could take the following actions:

1. Prioritize prevention and response to sexual harassment.
2. Ensure that training and prevention materials highlight that men and women are victims.
3. Continue investigating how sexual assault reporting affects separation risk.

Acknowledgments

We wish to acknowledge the valuable suggestions and advice we received in consultations with Beth Asch and Michael Mattock of the RAND Corporation. We are also grateful for the insightful and constructive critiques provided by two quality assurance reviewers, Anthony J. Rosellini of Boston University and James Hosek of RAND.

Abbreviations

CI	confidence interval
DMDC	Defense Manpower Data Center
DoD	U.S. Department of Defense
FY	fiscal year
GAO	U.S. Government Accountability Office
GLM	general linear model
OR	odds ratio
PTSD	posttraumatic stress disorder
RMWS	RAND Military Workplace Study
VA	U.S. Department of Veterans Affairs
WGRA	Workplace and Gender Relations Survey of Active Duty Members

CHAPTER ONE

Introduction

Sexual assault and sexual harassment can have harmful consequences for those who are targeted, including short- and long-term effects on psychological and physical health, associated and sometimes costly and time-consuming treatment needs, job dissatisfaction, and other hardships (Dichter and True, 2015; Fitzgerald, Drasgow, and Magley, 1999; Frayne et al., 1999; Turchik and Wilson, 2010; Willness, Steel, and Lee, 2007). In addition to consequences that are largely borne by the target of the abuse, sexual assault and sexual harassment may have deleterious and costly consequences for employers in general if the abuse results in higher turnover or low morale and productivity. In this chapter, we review the literature on these harmful effects.

Much of the literature on the effects of sexual assault and sexual harassment has been conducted in the civilian population. However, the military context is different in several ways that may make it difficult to generalize the civilian research to military populations. Unlike in the civilian world, active-duty service members generally cannot sue their employer for failing to correct hostile workplace environments, so damages awarded to victims of abuse are not among the costs borne by the U.S. Department of Defense (DoD) as a consequence of sexual assault or sexual harassment of service members.[1] More generally, service members are not covered by the protections of Title VII of the Civil Rights Act of 1964 (Pub. L. 88-352) and cannot pursue legal action to stop harassment or get restitution for harassment (Fitzgerald, Swan, and Fischer, 1995; Sagawa and Campbell, 1992). Furthermore, service members, unlike civilian workers, are generally unable to switch to a new employer at a time of their choosing. However, victims may choose to avoid extending their current military commitment, thus affecting military retention.

If sexual assault and sexual harassment decrease retention in the armed services, this could impose significant costs on DoD as a result of the high costs of recruiting and training new members, placing greater administrative and financial burden on the military. DoD has an interest in reducing costs, especially those that affect readiness, so we consider such costs in this report. Federal agencies have previously considered

---

[1] Civilian DoD employees can seek legal claims for sexual assault and sexual harassment.

separation costs; for instance, in 2011, the U.S. Government Accountability Office (GAO) estimated that the separation of 3,644 active-duty members who violated certain conduct policies in a five-year period beginning in 2004 cost DoD $193.3 million, $52,800 per separation, almost all of which was due to replacing these service members (GAO, 2011).

In this report, we seek to quantify the effects of sexual assault and sexual harassment on separations from the U.S. military and, by extension, the effects on military costs and readiness. Specifically, we examine all separations, whether these occurred because service members voluntarily chose not to re-enlist or continue their service as an officer or because they were discharged from the military for reasons other than their choice not to renew their commitment to serve. We consider the characteristics of observed separations and provide additional information regarding why these service members separated. In addition, we examine the reasons recorded for these separations and whether service members whose survey responses led us to classify them as having been sexually assaulted or sexually harassed were more likely to (1) leave the military of their own volition or (2) be discharged for reasons associated with their failure to meet expectations for their performance or conduct.[2]

To conduct these analyses, we drew on personnel records and the RAND Military Workplace Study (RMWS), a large-scale survey of sexual assault and sexual harassment experiences conducted in 2014 (see Morral, Gore, and Schell, 2014). Before describing these analyses and results, we first summarize previous research on the effects of sexual assault and sexual harassment among veterans and those still serving in the U.S. military.

Effects of Sexual Assault on Service Members

Previous research, discussed in this section, has documented multiple adverse outcomes, including poorer physical and mental health and negative workplace outcomes, associated with sexual assault among U.S. service members and veterans.[3]

---

[2]   In the results from the RMWS described in this report, reference to *sexual assault* is based on survey respondents' answers to questions about their experiences but does not reflect whether a sexual assault was substantiated by an investigation. In addition, reference to *sexual harassment* is also based on survey respondents' answers to questions about their experiences and does not reflect whether sexual harassment was substantiated by an investigation. Use of the terms *perpetrator* and *victim* in this report are not intended to presume the guilt or innocence of an individual.

[3]   Health and workplace outcomes are not always independent of each other. Thus, declining physical and mental health may lead to or exacerbate workplace challenges. Such problems may ultimately make continued service or employment untenable from both the employee and employer perspectives.

Health Outcomes

The health effects of experiencing sexual assault may contribute to workplace outcomes, including military separation. Research with U.S. military veterans has shown associations between multiple physical health symptoms and the experience of sexual assault during military service (Frayne et al., 1999; Sadler et al., 2004; Suris and Lind, 2008). This includes, for example, a greater number of reproductive, urological, neurological, gastrointestinal, and pulmonary symptoms among veterans who reported experiencing sexual assault while in the military compared with veterans who did not (Frayne et al., 1999). In addition, sexual assault and military sexual trauma during military service are associated with poorer psychological health outcomes among veterans, such as depression, anxiety, suicidal ideation, and posttraumatic stress disorder (PTSD) symptoms (Kimerling et al., 2010; Suris and Lind, 2008; Turchik and Wilson, 2010).[4] Initial research also suggests that psychological health symptoms might mediate the relationship between in-service sexual assault and post-service physical health symptoms (Smith et al., 2011).

Although studies assessing the association between sexual assault and health outcomes among those who have served in the military often use veteran samples, some research has considered the associations among those still on active duty. For example, lifetime sexual trauma, which includes experiences before and during military service, among active-duty male and female soldiers is related to a greater number of psychological and physical health symptoms among men and women (Martin et al., 2000; Smith et al., 2008). Similarly, a study of active-duty women found that those who reported experiencing sexual assault while in the military felt poorer health satisfaction and perceived that they had lower psychological well-being (Harned et al., 2002).

Workplace Outcomes and Separation

Relative to the number of studies examining the health correlates of sexual assault on service members, the research considering the effects of in-service sexual assault on military workplace outcomes has been limited. However, the research that has been conducted in this area suggests that sexual assault is associated with negative occupational outcomes and separation among military personnel. For example, in two studies utilizing semi-structured interviews with cohorts of 35 and 21 female veterans, participants noted that sexual assault contributed to premature separation or discharge from

---

[4] *Military sexual trauma* is a U.S. Department of Veterans Affairs (VA) self-report screening term that relates to the experience of sexual assault, sexual harassment, or both at any point during one's military service. The VA uses the military sexual trauma screen to identify veterans who may benefit from care, recovery services, and compensation claims. The term is not synonymous with *sexual assault* as used by DoD, which refers to a variety of penetrative and sexual contact crimes prohibited by military law. DoD employs separate programs for sexual assault and sexual harassment because law and policy require different responses. However, because the impacts to the individual are quite similar, the research studies referenced in this section include cohorts of personnel who indicated a history of experiencing sexual assault, who screened positive in the VA for military sexual trauma, or both.

the military (Dichter and True, 2015; Katz, Huffman, and Cojucar, 2017). In addition, Rosellini and colleagues (2017) conducted a study examining career outcomes among women in the U.S. Army and found that, compared with matched controls, those who had administratively recorded experiences of sexual assault victimization showed significantly higher odds of mental health treatment, suicide attempts, demotion, and attrition (Rosellini et al., 2017).[5] A study of active-duty men and women also found that those who experienced sexual assault and sexual harassment (with no study participants reporting sexual assault but not sexual harassment) reported poorer adjustment in work roles and social functioning than those who did not have these experiences (Murdoch et al., 2007).

Two studies examined adverse health and occupational outcomes associated with experiencing recent sexual trauma among men and women serving in the U.S. military (Millegan et al., 2015; Millegan et al., 2016). These studies made use of data collected as part of the Millennium Cohort Study, one of the largest prospective studies to be conducted with U.S. service members (Ryan et al., 2007). Data included participants' responses to questionnaires administered between 2001 and 2008, which included a baseline questionnaire and two follow-ups. In adjusted models that included demographics; historical sexual trauma; and service, behavioral, and health characteristics, women who experienced recent sexual assault had higher odds of reporting difficulties in work activities as a result of increased issues with emotional and physical health (Millegan et al., 2015; Millegan et al., 2016). Millegan and colleagues did not report analyses with these variables for men.[6]

Finally, in prior analyses of the data used in this report (Jaycox et al., 2015), service members who had experiences consistent with a sexual assault in the past year, based on survey responses, were found to be more likely than those without such experiences to report a desire to leave the military. Nearly half of all members who were sexually assaulted (46 percent), again based on classification using survey responses, indicated that the assault made it harder for them to perform their duties in the military. In addition, sampled members who separated from the military during the survey period were found to indicate significantly higher rates of past-year sexual assault expe-

---

[5]   The Rosellini et al. (2017) method of obtaining "administratively recorded sexual assault victimization" did not rely on official means of documenting sexual assault, relied only on the term *sexual assault* in a record to include it in the research, confounded sexual assault with military sexual trauma in some cases, and failed to include in the analyses a proportion of sexual assaults documented annually as restricted reports. As a result, the study may have inaccurately identified the odds of the outcomes characterized.

[6]   Notably, Millegan and colleagues used data from a population-based sample from 2000, and participants included in the analyses were older than the general military population. Because sexual assault appears to be more prevalent among younger than older adults, the analyses may have underestimated prevalence within the military (Millegan et al., 2015; Millegan et al., 2016). Furthermore, to assess the experience of sexual assault, participants were asked if they "suffered forced sexual relations or sexual assault" in the past three years. The use of items that were not behaviorally specific may have contributed to inaccurate estimates of sexual assault (Morral, Gore, and Schell, 2014).

riences (based on our classification of those experiences according to survey responses) than those who did not separate were, and these differences were not explained by differences in pay grade, service branch, or race/ethnicity (Ghosh-Dastidar et al., 2016).

Effects of Sexual Harassment on Service Members

More service members report experiencing sexual harassment than sexual assault (Millegan et al., 2015; Millegan et al., 2016; Morral, Gore, and Schell, 2015a), and, like sexual assault, the experience of sexual harassment appears to be associated with multiple negative effects (Willness, Steel, and Lee, 2007).

Health Outcomes

Research has shown that, among veterans, the experience of in-service sexual harassment is associated with various negative psychological effects, including depression, PTSD symptoms, and poorer general mental health, as well as a greater number of medical conditions (Street et al., 2007; Street et al., 2008). Similarly, research with active-duty personnel has shown multiple negative health consequences of in-service sexual harassment, such as lower health satisfaction and psychological well-being (Fitzgerald, Drasgow, and Magley, 1999).

Workplace Outcomes and Separation

Several studies have considered the workplace outcomes, which encompass perceptions of and behavioral intentions in the workplace, associated with in-service sexual harassment among military samples. A meta-analysis found that sexual harassment was associated with lower supervisor satisfaction, coworker satisfaction, work satisfaction, and organizational commitment for military and nonmilitary samples, and sexual harassment had a stronger negative impact on work satisfaction among military than nonmilitary personnel (Willness, Steel, and Lee, 2007). In addition, when examining turnover among women in the military, Sims, Drasgow, and Fitzgerald (2005) found that lower supervisor satisfaction, coworker satisfaction, work satisfaction, and organizational commitment were associated with increased risk of military turnover, but across models, sexual harassment predicted higher risk of turnover after controlling for each of these facets of job satisfaction and commitment. As noted previously, the authors conducted analyses only with service women, so the extent to which their results apply to men is not clear. Also, to assess sexual harassment, they used responses to the DoD Sexual Experiences Questionnaire (Fitzgerald et al., 1999), and issues with the measure of sexual harassment (i.e., combining sexual harassment with other behaviors) may have influenced participant responses and subsequent results (for additional discussion of previous measurement limitations, see Farris et al., 2014).

In addition to considering sexual assault, Millegan and colleagues assessed the potential effects of sexual harassment among service members within the Millennium Cohort Study (Millegan et al., 2015; Millegan et al., 2016). Adjusted models showed that service women who experienced recent sexual harassment had higher odds of reporting difficulties in work activities as a result of issues with emotional and physical health. (Analyses with these variables were not reported for men.) Analyses also showed that service women who experienced recent sexual harassment had higher odds of experiencing a demotion. Among service men, experiencing sexual harassment was associated with poorer mental and physical health, demotion, and separation, compared with men who did not report experiencing such harassment (Millegan et al., 2016).[7]

Finally, in earlier analyses of some of the data used in this report, Farris et al. (2015) found that, among surveyed service members who indicated sexual harassment experiences (again, based on our classification of those experiences according to survey responses), large proportions indicated that the sexual harassment resulted in workplace arguments or reportedly damaged unit cohesion (53 percent), made it difficult for them to complete their work (50 percent), or compromised the unit's mission effectiveness and productivity (48 percent).

Organization of This Report

Previous research suggests that experiencing sexual assault or sexual harassment has multiple negative effects for service members. The remaining chapters in this report describe analyses conducted using 2014 RMWS survey data to assess military separation following service member experience of sexual assault or sexual harassment, as based on service member responses to the RMWS survey. Chapter Two describes our analytic approach to estimating the effects of sexual assault and sexual harassment on military separation. Chapter Three provides the results of our analyses, and Chapter Four provides conclusions and recommendations based on our analyses.

---

[7] As discussed previously, characteristics of the samples and measures may have influenced assessments of sexual harassment in these studies.

CHAPTER TWO

Approach to Estimating the Effects of Sexual Assault and Sexual Harassment on Separation from the Military

In 2014, the RAND Corporation conducted the RMWS (Morral, Gore, and Schell, 2014, 2015a, 2015b, 2016), at the time one of the largest surveys of sexual assault and sexual harassment experiences in the military. Among the active component, 477,513 service members were invited to participate, and 145,300 completed the web-administered survey. In this chapter, we describe the design of analyses that draw from both the RMWS data and military personnel records to assess career effects of experiencing sexual assault or sexual harassment. This research was reviewed and approved by institutional review boards at both RAND and DoD.

Data Sources and Sample Characteristics

RMWS Survey Data

Although the RMWS included a small number of respondents from the reserve component and from the U.S. Coast Guard, our analyses in this report focus exclusively on results from the active component of the four DoD services (Army, Navy, Air Force, and Marine Corps). Details of the overall study design can be found in Volume 1 of this report series (Morral, Gore, and Schell, 2014). Members of the active component were randomized to receive (1) the newer RMWS measures of sexual assault and sexual harassment (*the RAND form*), (2) an abbreviated RMWS form that assessed sexual assault but did not fully assess sexual harassment, or (3) the measures that had previously been used to assess each construct (*the prior form*), which was last used by DoD in the 2012 Workplace and Gender Relations Survey of Active Duty Members (WGRA).[1] The data analyzed here combine the RMWS and prior form measurements

---

[1] Both newer (as of 2014) and older measures were administered to allow a direct comparison between the two instruments. This is helpful for maintaining interpretable time-series data on sexual assault in the military. Some respondents were randomized to receive only some of the sexual harassment items in an effort to reduce the overall response burden of the survey.

of sexual assault, but not sexual harassment, to allow for a larger analytic sample.[2] In total, we included 145,300 RMWS active-component respondents in the analysis of sexual assault and 95,960 respondents in the analysis of sexual harassment.

Respondents were counted as being exposed to a past-year sexual assault if they indicated a past-year "unwanted sexual contact," the prior form's measure of sexual assault, or if they were counted on the RAND form as having experienced a past-year sexual assault. Follow-up questions about the circumstances and consequences of sexual assaults were asked only of respondents who were given the RAND form (n = 115,759), of which there were 2,224 respondents who were classified as experiencing a past-year sexual assault.[3] As published in earlier reports, we estimated that 1.5 percent of active-component DoD service members experienced sexual assault in the prior year (see, for example, Morral, Gore, and Schell, 2015a). We used this subset of respondents who experienced a sexual assault to conduct secondary analyses of the association between characteristics of the sexual assault and separation from the military. Specifically, we looked at the type of sexual assault (penetrative, nonpenetrative, or attempted), the number of assaults in the past year, and whether the victim indicated on the survey that they had reported the assault to the military authorities.

Respondents were counted as having experienced a past-year incident of sexual harassment on the basis of their responses to items on the RAND form, which assessed behavioral indicators of sexual harassment but did not require service members to correctly label any such incidents as "sexual harassment." There were 6,866 respondents who were classified as having experienced sexual harassment in the past year. As published in earlier reports, we estimated that 8.9 percent of active-component DoD service members experienced sexual harassment in the prior year (Morral, Gore, and Schell, 2015a).[4]

Personnel Records

The Defense Manpower Data Center (DMDC) provided personnel data on the full sample frame of 1,317,561 active-component service members for use in these analyses. The sample frame included all enlisted active-component personnel and officers with a rank of O-6 (colonel) or below as of April 2014.

Our primary outcome variable was separation from the military within 28 months from when the sample frame was drawn (i.e., separation between April 2014 and September 2016, as recorded in the monthly DMDC Work Experience File). By *separation from the military*, we specifically refer to the members of the active-component sample

---

[2] Rates of sexual harassment found on the prior form and the RMWS are reported together in Volume 2 of this report series (Morral, Gore, and Schell, 2015a). A detailed discussion of differences in the coverage of these measures is found in Volume 4, Chapter Eight (Morral, Gore, and Schell, 2016).

[3] This describes the sample we used to produce the estimates in this report, not the estimates for the population.

[4] This describes the sample we used to produce the estimates in this report, not the estimates for the population.

frame who separated entirely from the military. Those who simply transitioned from the active component to the reserve component were not treated as separating from the military.[5] There were 217,410 service members, or roughly 17 percent of the sample frame, who separated from the military by this definition over the 28-month period. Table 2.1 displays the numbers of service members who were retained and who separated over this period, by pay grade category and gender. This provides baseline information regarding separations.

Figure 2.1 illustrates the association between years of service as of April 2014 and percentage remaining in the military among members of the sample frame over the subsequent 28-month period. There is a strong correlation between years of service and retention for officers and enlisted members. After an initial wave of attrition at the end of service members' initial terms of service, retention steadily grows as service members near the 20-year mark, when many can receive their full retirement benefits. Thereafter, retention declines sharply in each subsequent year. This sudden reduction (seen by the lower position of the blue and red markers at year 18 compared with year 17) appears to occur in year 18, rather than in year 20, in the figure because years of service was measured at the beginning of the more than two-year period over which separations were observed.

Table 2.1
Separations from the Military During the 28-Month Observation Period, by Pay Grade Category and Gender

Pay Grade Category and Gender	Remained in the Military After 28 Months	Left the Military After 28 Months	Percentage Remaining
Officers			
Men	169,105	25,830	87
Women	34,016	4,479	88
Total	203,121	30,309	87
Enlisted			
Men	766,704	158,431	83
Women	130,326	28,670	82
Total	897,030	187,101	83

NOTE: Appendix A contains a further breakdown of separation rates by service, pay grade category, and gender.

---

[5] The same pattern of results described here was found when we used *separation from the active component* as the outcome measure. This measure treats those who transitioned from the active component to the reserve component as separated. Because the results were comparable, and because separation from the military may represent an outcome of greater concern than separation from the active component, we report here just the results for separation from the military.

Figure 2.1
Active-Component Retention, by Years of Service at the Start of the 28-Month Observation Period

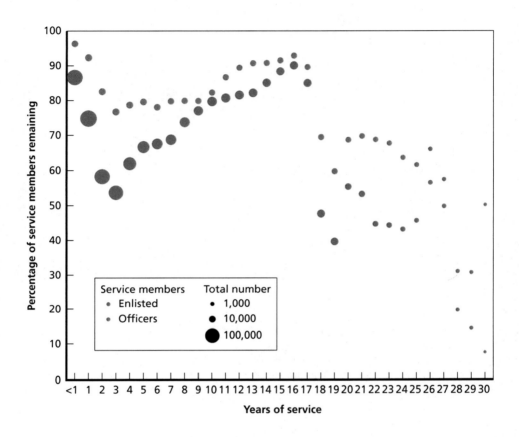

Although separation from the military was the primary outcome variable that we investigated, in secondary analyses, we examined whether those who were sexually assaulted were more likely to separate voluntarily or to separate involuntarily for any of a set of reasons that we refer to as *discharges for failure to adhere to standards or expectations*. These secondary analyses addressed characteristics of service member separations, thereby providing additional information regarding the nature of the separations. The ten most-common discharge codes that we counted as indicating a failure to adhere to standards or expectations were, in decreasing order of frequency,

1. discharges for drug offenses
2. commission of a serious offense
3. unqualified for active duty (other)
4. failure to meet weight or body fat standards
5. unsatisfactory performance
6. discreditable incidents

7. failure to meet minimum qualifications
8. early release (insufficient retainability)
9. pattern of minor disciplinary infractions
10. alcoholism.

The complete list of discharge codes is found in Appendix B.

The person-level predictors of separation from the military that we used in the present analyses are as follows:

- gender
- age
- race
- ethnicity
- educational level (six categories)
- marital status
- number of dependents
- service branch
- pay grade (seven levels)
- location (state or country)
- occupational group (20 categories)
- months deployed in career
- months deployed in past 12 months
- date of commission or enlistment
- source of commission or enlistment
- active-duty end date
- months of active-duty service (lifetime)
- Armed Forces Qualification Test score
- strength accounting code
- time in current pay grade (normalized)
- time in previous pay grade (normalized).

Statistically significant bivariate results led us to incorporate the selected characteristics into analyses. Specifically, we included these characteristics in analyses to account for their possible associations with separation, either voluntary or involuntary, from the military. Inclusion of the characteristics allowed us to assess the effects of sexual assault and sexual harassment (both based on our classifications of individuals by survey responses) on separation above and beyond the effects of these characteristics. Values for the predictors were determined as of the time the sample frame was drawn (April 2014), with four exceptions. Active-duty end date was established as of September 2016. We determined an individual's strength accounting code (an indication of the member's current availability to report for duty), time in current pay grade, and time in previous pay grade as of September 2013, roughly at the beginning of the 12-month period over which sexual assault and sexual harassment experiences were assessed in the RMWS. Because we wanted to estimate the effect of sexual assault and sexual harassment on separation, it was important that the predictors of separation that we included in our models were not themselves affected by any past-year sexual assault or sexual harassment. For example, if someone was in the hospital in April 2014 because of a sexual assault that occurred a month earlier, that could be reflected in a strength accounting code indicating hospitalization. Similarly, although sexual assault and sexual harassment experiences should not affect promotion decisions, we erred on the side of caution by calculating time in current pay grade (and therefore time in prior grade) as of September 2013 as well, because no sexual assault or sexual harassment experiences measured as past-year events on the RMWS could have affected members' pay grade as of that date.

Time in current pay grade and time in previous pay grade were normalized using the amount of time others at the same pay grade in the sample frame had spent in that grade. This process places values on a common scale, facilitating comparisons. Specifically, for each individual i in pay grade p, we calculated the time in current pay grade z-score as

$$z_{ip} = \frac{t_{ip} - \overline{t_p}}{s_p},$$

where t_{ip} is the time the individual has spent in the pay grade, $\overline{t_p}$ is the average time others in pay grade p have served in that grade, and s_p is the standard deviation of time spent in the pay grade. Time in previous pay grade is similar but assesses whether an individual spent more or less time in his or her previous pay grade than his or her current pay-grade peers spent in their prior pay grades.

Statistical Methods

The effect of sexual assault on the probability of separation was estimated within a survey-weighted logistic regression model. We sought to address the possibilities, however, that the relationship between the covariates and the probability of separation may be complex and nonlinear (e.g., the relationship between length of service and separation could be substantially different for different pay grades, and the association may not be linear within any pay grade), and these nonlinearities might be difficult to capture in a general linear model (GLM) framework. To address this, we first used a nonlinear machine-learning algorithm to predict separation for each individual in the full population based on the person-level variables listed earlier.[6] The predicted probability of separation from this initial, nonlinear model was incorporated as a separate offset term in the GLM used to estimate the effect of sexual assault on separation so that the GLM would capture any nonlinearities in the relationship between the covariates and the outcomes.

This two-staged modeling approach offers several advantages. The first-stage model identifies risk of separation using the entire population of active-component service members rather than just WGRA respondents. It is a nonlinear model that identifies interactions between predictors and other nonlinear relationships automatically. This ensures optimal prediction of separation risk on the basis of the demographic and service characteristics. However, this type of modeling is not especially useful for establishing the effect of a particular predictor (such as sexual assault or sexual harassment exposure) on the outcome. The second-stage model seeks to answer how much better we can predict separation with information on sexual assault or sexual harassment exposure over and above the information about separation risk from the first-stage model. Because it uses sexual assault or sexual harassment information, this model can be run only on WGRA respondents. We incorporate their predicted risk from the first-stage model, so we can evaluate how much sexual assault or sexual harassment information improves upon the first-stage model estimates.

Initial Nonlinear Model

We estimated an initial nonlinear model on all 1.3 million active-component members who were in the April 2014 sample frame for the RMWS. We used generalized boosted regression (see Ridgeway, 2018) with four-way interactions to fit an adaptive, nonlinear regression of separations on the 21 person-level predictors listed earlier. We assessed optimal model complexity using fivefold cross-validation, and we selected the final model as the iteration that minimized the cross-validated error of prediction. These models were fit using a logit link and loss function and produced the predicted log odds of separation for each individual.

The relative influence column in Table 2.2 indicates the proportion of deviance reduction in the separation outcome associated with each predictor in the final model. As is evident from Figure 2.1, separation probability was highly, and nonlinearly, associated with years of service. It is not surprising, therefore, that months of active-duty service was one of the strongest predictors. Similarly, those whose current contracts were set to expire within the 28-month follow-up period were much more likely to separate than were those with longer service commitments.

---

[6] This involved use of generalized boosted regressions. These can be used for prediction from a large number of variables while also permitting flexible, nonlinear relationships between variables. They provide a more flexible approach to modeling than do parametric logistic regression models that assume that variables are linear and additive on the log-odds scale (McCaffrey, Ridgeway, and Morral, 2004).

Table 2.2
Contributions of Predictors in the Initial Nonlinear Model of Separations

Predictor	Relative Influence (%)
Months of active-duty service	25.41
Active-duty end date	18.77
Age	10.31
Location (state or country)	8.77
Pay grade	8.36
Time in current pay grade (normalized)	6.27
Service branch	4.79
Date of commission or enlistment	4.53
Occupational group (20 categories)	3.43
Source of commission or enlistment	2.67
AFQT score percentile	1.39
Time in previous pay grade (normalized)	1.31
Strength accounting code	0.79
Race	0.78
Months deployed in career	0.50
Educational level (six categories)	0.50
Ethnicity	0.36
Months deployed in past 12 months	0.33
Number of dependents	0.31
Marital status	0.24
Gender	0.17

NOTE: *Relative influence* is an effect size measure that describes the proportion of any reduction in a model's loss function that is attributable to each model variable. For a Gaussian outcome, this would be the proportion of reduced squared error attributable to each variable (Friedman, 2001). AFQT = Armed Forces Qualification Test.

General Linear Model

To assess the associations between (1) sexual assault and sexual harassment and (2) separation, we used a conventional logistic regression. These models were estimated using all the respondents to the RMWS (N = 145,300). Specifically, we used SAS *PROC SurveyLogistic* with sampling and nonresponse weights, described in more depth later in this chapter. We also included the predicted log-odds of separation from the machine-learning model fit to the full population as a model offset in order to capture the non-linear relationships between the covariates and the outcome.[7]

We ran separate models, including sexual assault and sexual harassment during fiscal year (FY) 2014 as predictors, using the measures from the RMWS. We also included the following 11 covariates in the GLM logistic regression:

1. end date of current term (trichotomized: during the 28-month observation period, after, or unknown)
2. age
3. pay grade
4. location (state or country)
5. time in current pay grade (normalized)
6. date of commission or enlistment
7. source of commission or enlistment
8. strength accounting code
9. race
10. ethnicity
11. number of dependents.

These covariates were a subset of the broader list of covariates used in the machine-learning model. We used a subset of all available covariates because (1) the full model contained collinearities that prevent GLM estimation, and (2) it was not parsimonious to estimate a model containing all of the available variables. We selected these 11 covariates because they provided the best GLM fit of all investigated subsets, as judged by the Akaike information criterion (see Bozdogan, 1987). In general, the model results are not sensitive to the selection of covariates in the GLM. This is due to the inclusion of the nonlinear term that captures the relationship between these covariates and separations estimated on the full military population. Thus, the GLM logistic regression including all 11 covariates showed excellent prediction of separations (area under the curve = 0.83); however, a model omitting the covariates showed an identical area under the curve and a nearly identical estimate of the effect of sexual assault. In addition to these 11 covariates, we included gender as a covariate, and it interacted

---

[7] These analyses seek to address what sexual assault and sexual harassment information can explain about separations over and above what demographic and service variables can explain. Alternative analyses, such as conducting logistic regression once with the term used to establish what the demographic and service variables can explain and then another time without the term, would no longer address the question of interest. We include the top predictors in the first-stage model in this second-stage model for technical reasons. In brief, the first-stage model might have used information about sexual assault or sexual harassment risk found in the demographic or service variables. Adding the top predictors from the first-stage model to the second-stage model allows the sexual assault or sexual harassment predictor to reclaim variance in the outcome that the first-stage model captured. The results are insensitive to the inclusion of these covariates.

with sexual assault in some additional models. We did this so that we could investigate the possibility of differential effects of sexual assault and sexual harassment by gender.

After estimating the effects of sexual assault and sexual harassment within a logistic regression model, we described those effects by computing marginal effects projected to the full population. To compute standard errors for these marginal effects, we used a resampling procedure. Specifically, we computed an estimate of the number of separations associated with sexual assault by multiplying the total number of sexual assaults by the difference between the observed separation rates among those who were sexually assaulted and the model-based estimate of their separation rates had they not been assaulted. Correct confidence intervals (CIs) require that we account for uncertainty both in the total number of members with past-year sexual assaults and in the estimates of the effect of sexual assault on separation rates. This was accomplished by using a bootstrap technique appropriate for complex survey data (Rust and Rao, 1996). Within each bootstrap sample, we estimated the total number of sexual assaults, along with the model used to estimate the separation rates. We used these estimates, in turn, to estimate the number of separations that were associated with sexual assault in each bootstrap sample.

We generated 1,000 bootstrap samples and constructed CIs using the 2.5th and 97.5th percentiles of the bootstrapped distribution.

Analytic Weights

Initial analyses were conducted using the standard RMWS analytic weights (see Morral, Gore, and Schell, 2016). These weights take into account both the survey design and survey nonresponse, and, by using them, we seek to make the analytic sample representative of the full population for the variables that were available at the time the survey was completed. However, these initial analyses demonstrated that the RMWS weights did not make the weighted sample representative of the broader population in their probability of separating from the military in the subsequent months. Specifically, the weighted survey respondents were substantially less likely to separate from service than the broader population that the weighted sample was designed to represent, while survey nonrespondents were more likely than respondents to subsequently leave the military.

To ensure that the sample was representative of the population on the key outcome of interest for this study, we adjusted the standard RMWS weights to increase the weight given to respondents who subsequently left the military. This was done using an additional poststratification step that included information about subsequent separation from service. Specifically, the separation-adjusted RMWS weights ensure that the weighted sample has the correct separation rate within each combination of gender, pay grade, and service. For a further discussion of the assumptions and statistical methods used for nonresponse weighting in this survey, see Morral, Gore, and Schell (2016).

CHAPTER THREE

Findings on the Effects of Sexual Assault and Sexual Harassment on Separation from the Military

In this chapter, we describe the results of analyses estimating the effects of sexual assault and sexual harassment on separation from the military. We begin with a description of findings involving the effects of sexual assault on male and female service member separation, and we also consider the associations between characteristics of the sexual assault experiences and separation. We then describe the associations between sexual harassment (and characteristics of sexual harassment) and separation from the military.

Association Between Past-Year Sexual Assault and Separation from the Military

Experiencing sexual assault appears to be strongly associated with separation from military service. The logistic regression model estimated that the odds of separating from the military within a 28-month period were 2.03 times greater among those who were classified (based on their survey responses) as having been sexually assaulted during FY 2014, compared with those who were not, after controlling for the covariates described in Chapter Two (95% CI: 1.50–2.70). When analyzed separately, women (odds ratio [OR] = 1.72; 95% CI: 1.49–1.98) and men (OR = 2.35; 95% CI: 1.41–3.92) who were assaulted had comparably elevated odds of military separation, after controlling for all other characteristics. The difference in ORs between women and men was not statistically significant. Overall, these results suggest that sexual assault increased the odds of separating for both men and women.

Overall, we estimate that 5,600 (95% CI: 4,600–7,000) of the 21,000 (95% CI: 19,100–23,000) service members who were estimated to have been sexually assaulted in FY 2014 left the military in the subsequent 28-month period.[1] Of course, some of

---

[1] This estimate of 21,000 (95% CI: 19,300–23,300) service members who experienced a sexual assault in FY 2014 is slightly higher than the estimate of 20,300 (95% CI: 18,200–22,400) published in Morral, Gore, and Schell (2015a). This difference occurs because the current estimates used weights that take into account subsequent military separations. The original RMWS weights did not accurately weight respondents to look like the

these service members would have left the military even if they had not been sexually assaulted. Our analyses suggest, however, that among these sexual assault victims, there were 2,000 (95% CI: 1,100–3,100) more separations than would be predicted had these individuals not been assaulted. In other words, there were an estimated 2,000 separations associated with sexual assault.

Previous analyses suggested that sexual assaults in the military occur more often against service members who are younger and more junior ranking (Morral, Gore, and Schell, 2015a), and these characteristics may also describe the service members most likely to separate from the military in the short term. Indeed, we estimate that, even if the service members who were sexually assaulted (based on classification according to survey responses) in FY 2014 had not been assaulted, they would have had a probability of separating over the 28-month period (0.17 percent; 95% CI: 0.16–0.19) that was marginally higher than the separation probability of those who were not assaulted (again, based on classification according to survey responses) (0.16 percent; 95% CI: 0.16–0.17). However, the actual rate of separations among personnel whose survey responses suggested they were sexually assaulted was 0.27 percent (95% CI: 0.23–0.32)—a substantial increase from their expected rate had they not been sexually assaulted (0.17 percent). In other words, those who were sexually assaulted appear to separate from the military at a higher rate than would be expected had they not been assaulted.

Association Between Characteristics of Sexual Assault and Separation

We next conducted a series of secondary analyses to examine whether specific features of sexual assaults were associated with separation from the military, addressing number of assaults, penetrative or nonpenetrative assaults, and whether an official report was filed. These analyses used data from the 2,224 RAND-form respondents who experienced an assault and received questions about the circumstances of the sexual assault. Thus, these analyses have much lower statistical power than the findings reported on the entire sample of RMWS respondents.

Among these respondents whose survey responses suggested they experienced any sexual assault, we estimated the effects of the number of assaults during FY 2014 on the likelihood of separating. The service members whose survey responses suggested they experienced two or more separate sexual assaults had significantly higher odds of separating relative to members whose survey responses suggested they experienced a single assault during the year (OR = 1.94; 95% CI: 1.33–2.83).

Those whose survey responses suggested they experienced a penetrative assault appeared to have higher odds of separation than those whose survey responses sug-

population in terms of the number of separations occurring over the 28-month interval. People who went on to leave the military were underrepresented in the survey and were more likely to be sexually assaulted. Making the sample representative of the population on this variable increased the population estimate of sexual assaults.

gested their assaults were not penetrative, after controlling for other predictors of separation (OR = 1.37; 95% CI: 0.79–2.37). However, this effect was not statistically significant. Similarly, we found that, compared with not filing such a report, filing an official report of a sexual assault with the military was not significantly associated with a change in the odds of separation (OR = 0.84; 95% CI: 0.49–1.43).[2]

Association Between Sexual Assault and a Discharge for Failure to Adhere to Standards or Expectations

In addition to predicting the probability of separating, we looked at the type of separation among those who separated, thereby assessing additional contextual information regarding the separations. Among the 15,603 service members who separated over the 28-month period that we examined, 1,919 had discharge codes that we classified as relating to a failure to adhere to standards or expectations (e.g., alcohol abuse, crime, insubordination, and inability to achieve minimal standards; see Chapter Two). We found that service members with FY 2014 sexual assaults had lower odds of separating with a discharge for *failure to adhere to standards or expectations* compared with those who did not experience sexual assault in FY 2014 (OR = 0.38; 95% CI: 0.19–0.78). Thus, these sexual assault victims were highly likely to *choose* to leave the military and were less likely than their peers to be discharged as a result of performance or behavior problems. This effect was significantly stronger among male sexual assault victims than among female victims.[3]

Association Between Past-Year Sexual Harassment and Separation from the Military

Like experiencing sexual assault, experiencing sexual harassment appears to be strongly associated with separation from military service. Service members whose survey responses indicated that they were sexually harassed had odds of separating that were 1.70 times greater than those whose survey responses indicated that they were not sexually harassed (95% CI: 1.42–2.04). When we analyzed genders separately, we found that women who experienced sexual harassment had attrition odds that were 1.50 times greater than those of other women (95% CI: 1.34–1.68), and men who experienced sexual harassment showed attrition odds that were 1.91 times greater than those of other men (95% CI: 1.48–2.47). The difference in the ORs between men and

---

[2] An official report regarding possible experiences of sexual assault could have been a restricted report, an unrestricted report, or both.

[3] This effect is found as a significant interaction between gender and sexual assault exposure. We do not report the OR on the interaction term, because it is difficult to interpret by itself.

women was not statistically significant, which suggests that the effect of sexual harassment on separation is not substantially different between men and women.

Overall, we estimate that 28,200 (95% CI: 24,300–32,800) of 117,000 (95% CI: 110,500–123,500) service members who appeared to have experienced sexual harassment in FY 2014 separated from the service over the 28-month period that we examined. Accounting for other service member characteristics that may be associated with separation, we estimate that there were approximately 8,000 (95% CI: 5,100–11,200) more separations of sexually harassed service members than would be predicted had these individuals not been sexually harassed. Exposure to FY 2014 sexual harassment, based on classification according to survey responses, was associated with an increase in the probability of separation from 0.17 percent (95% CI: 0.16–0.19) to 0.24 percent (95% CI: 0.21–0.27).

Our findings show strong associations between both sexual harassment and sexual assault in separate analyses. Some of the separation risk associated with sexual harassment could, therefore, be due to sexual assaults experienced by the same individuals. To clarify the interpretation of these effects, we created a variable that indicated individuals who experienced sexual harassment without experiencing any sexual assault (again, using survey responses to classify individuals according to these experiences). We then estimated a logistic regression model that included both sexual assault and sexual harassment without sexual assault as predictors. These analyses found that both sexual assault and sexual harassment without sexual assault were significant predictors of separation in a model controlling for other covariates. In this model, experiencing sexual assault was associated with odds of separating over the period that were 1.80 times greater than for members who were not sexually assaulted (95% CI: 1.28–2.53); experiencing sexual harassment without sexual assault was associated with odds of separating that were 1.63 times greater than those who were not sexually harassed (95% CI: 1.35–1.96).

Association Between Characteristics of Sexual Harassment and Separation

We investigated whether certain types or characteristics of sexual harassment were more likely to be associated with separations than others, using data from 6,866 respondents who indicated experiences consistent with sexual harassment in FY 2014 and who received questions regarding the circumstances of the sexual harassment. When we examined the potential influence of experiencing sexual harassment across people and settings, our analyses showed that service member odds of separation were more than 50-percent higher when experiences of sexual harassment involved multiple people or settings rather than a single person or setting (OR = 1.54; 95% CI: 1.16–2.06).[4] However, the odds of separation did not significantly differ by the status of the harasser (i.e., supervisor, peer, or subordinate), by whether the respondent spoke to a supervisor

---

[4] There is insufficient statistical power to perform subgroup comparisons, such as by gender, for this analysis.

about the problem, or by whether the respondent expressed satisfaction or dissatisfaction with the result of such a supervisor discussion. Notably, lower statistical power for these analyses may have limited our ability to detect effects, if present.

Association Between Sexual Harassment and a Discharge for Failure to Adhere to Standards or Expectations

As we did with sexual assaults, we examined discharge type among the 8,909 survey respondents who separated over the 28-month period and for whom sexual harassment experiences were assessed. This analysis found no significant evidence that discharge type was associated with sexual harassment. The odds of a discharge for *failure to adhere to standards or expectations* for those who were sexually harassed were 1.40 times greater than for those not sexually harassed (95% CI: 0.98–1.99).

CHAPTER FOUR

Conclusions and Recommendations

Using a representative sample of all service members in the active component as of April 2014, we examined whether exposure to sexual assault or sexual harassment in FY 2014 was associated with measurable effects on service members' separation from the U.S. military. We found that, of the roughly 98,000 members who separated from the military over the ensuing 28-month period, 2,000 of these losses appeared to be associated with experiences of sexual assault in FY 2014, and 8,000 of the losses were associated with sexual harassment in that year, although some of these 8,000 were the service members whose separations were also associated with sexual assault. That is, after controlling for all other characteristics of service members, we estimate that 2 percent of all military separations over a 28-month period were associated with sexual assault in FY 2014, and 8 percent of all separations were associated with sexual harassment.

It is worth noting that these are the separations during the observation period (essentially FYs 2015–2016) that were associated with just the sexual assaults or sexual harassment occurring in FY 2014. There is an unknown number of additional separations during the observation period that were associated with sexual assaults or sexual harassment that occurred either before or after FY 2014. Thus, the percentage of all separations within the period that might be attributable to prior sexual assault or sexual harassment is likely to be considerably higher than the percentages presented here, which were restricted to events in a single year.

In this chapter, we consider implications of this finding and provide recommendations on how DoD might use this information to assess and prevent unnecessary losses.

Separations Associated with Sexual Assault and Sexual Harassment Are Costly for the Services and the Members

Costs of personnel losses vary depending on the service member's service branch, years of service, and career specialty; whether the service is growing or shrinking; and many other factors. Moreover, although our analyses suggest that sexual assault and sexual harassment were associated with a considerable number of separations over a 28-month period, they do not indicate how much longer members would have served had they not been assaulted or harassed. Therefore, the exact costs of the personnel losses highlighted in our analyses are unclear. However, because the minimum re-enlistment period is typically two years, the services are losing at least 16,000 manpower years prematurely, and probably much more than this, as a result of separations associated with sexual assault and sexual harassment.[1] Furthermore, recruitment and training costs associated with replacing these service members are being shifted to an earlier time than would have been required had the services retained these individuals, thereby placing greater administrative and financial burden on the military.

While the effects of sexual assault and sexual harassment impose costs on the U.S. military, the active-duty victims of sexual assault and sexual harassment who separate from the military also incur considerable costs. Although compensation varies over time and across service members, the compensation that individuals receive while in the military is often higher than what they would receive in a comparable position in the civilian workforce (see, for example, Goldberg, 2001; Mattock et al., 2014). In addition, military compensation is weighted toward benefits received postretirement, or deferred payments (Military Compensation and Retirement Modernization Commission, 2015). Therefore, by separating before serving 20 years, service members forgo the opportunity to receive substantial postretirement compensation. Overall, members who separate from service because of sexual assault or sexual harassment are likely forgoing considerable compensation relative to continuing their service; indeed, some victims likely give up hundreds of thousands of dollars in lifetime earnings (see Figure 2.1 for information on when service members separate from the military).

Separations Associated with Sexual Assault Appear to Be Voluntary

Higher separation rates among those who were sexually assaulted or sexually harassed could be voluntary or involuntary. That is, these members may have preferred to leave the service, or they may have been discharged by the services for cause, such as alcoholism, crime, insubordination, failure to meet minimum requirements, or mental health problems. We labeled these causes *discharges for failure to adhere to standards or expectations*. Our results strongly suggest that separations following sexual assaults are more likely to be voluntary than involuntary for both men and women, and this tendency to leave voluntarily is even greater for men.

Although we did not find a significant association between sexual harassment and voluntary separations, sexual harassment has nearly as strong an association with an individual's likelihood of separating as does sexual assault. In addition, we did not find any statistically significant evidence that the type of separation for those who experi-

---

[1]   At least 8,000 service members chose to separate, rather than re-enlist, for reasons associated with sexual harassment. Re-enlistment periods are typically at least two years in length, so these separations likely deprived the military of at least 16,000 person-years of service.

enced sexual harassment differed from those who experienced assaults. These results suggest that high separation rates after service members experience sexual assaults are not primarily due to the services discharging members for cause. This also suggests that prevention efforts should be focused on reducing sexual assault and sexual harassment, given that they are both associated with separations.

Sexual Assault and Harassment Are Associated with Larger Numbers of Men Separating from the Services Than of Women

In FY 2014, we estimated that active-component women were about five times more likely to be sexually assaulted than men were and about 3.25 times more likely to be sexually harassed (Morral, Gore, and Schell, 2014). However, because there were nearly six times as many men as women in the active component, this meant that slightly more men than women were sexually assaulted, and the preponderance of those who were sexually harassed were men. In the present study, when comparing outcomes by gender, we found no evidence that the effect of sexual assault and sexual harassment on separation was significantly different for men relative to women.

Taken together, these observations imply that sexual assault and sexual harassment are associated with substantially larger numbers of separations of men than women, although such abuse affects a larger proportion of women than of men. We highlight this implication because sexual harassment in the military—and, to a lesser extent, sexual assault—is frequently thought of as a problem affecting women. This is correct in that a typical woman is more likely than a typical man to experience sexual harassment. However, men also experience sexual harassment, and the net effect of sexual harassment on readiness in the services is strongly determined by the sexual harassment of men or by factors associated with the sexual harassment of men.

Sexual Harassment Alone Is Associated with Increased Separations

Most sexual assaults of members in the military involve unwanted touching by a coworker, and some of these assaults might also include instances of sexual harassment.[2] This raises the possibility that the association we found between sexual harassment and elevated separation rates merely reflects the fact that many who were harassed were also assaulted, and those who were assaulted separate at higher rates. We ruled this possibility out, however, by performing analyses showing that members who were sexually harassed but not sexually assaulted also had an elevated risk of separation. Indeed, the

---

[2]   Unwanted sexual touching that rises to the level of sexual assault would automatically count as severe. It need not be pervasive to qualify as sexual harassment. This unwanted touching can take place off duty and away from a military facility, and it would still count as sexual harassment if done by a coworker.

effect of sexual harassment was quite similar whether we included or excluded individuals who were also assaulted.

This observation highlights that sexual harassment itself is a serious threat to readiness, independently of its frequent association with sexual assault. This is consistent with prior research (Murdoch et al., 2006), including research that has found that the experience of sexual harassment may undermine a service member's confidence that the military can provide a safe and supportive workplace (Schneider, Swan, and Fitzgerald, 1997). Whereas civilians—including DoD civilian employees—are covered by Title VII of the Civil Rights Act of 1964 (Pub. L. 88-352) and can pursue legal action against their employers if the workplace is not safe from unlawful harassment (Fitzgerald, Swan, and Fischer, 1995; Sagawa and Campbell, 1992), Title VII does not apply to uniformed military personnel, so this response strategy is not available to active-duty service members (Sagawa and Campbell, 1992). Furthermore, service members, unlike civilian workers, are generally unable to switch to a new employer at a time of their choosing. However, victims may choose to avoid extending their current military commitment, thus affecting military retention.

Estimates of Separations Associated with Sexual Harassment and Assault May Be Underestimates

The total number of separations associated with sexual assault and sexual harassment that we estimated in this report likely underestimates the size of the problem. Several factors cause this. First, we examined only separations that occurred in a 28-month period. Some members who were sexually assaulted or sexually harassed in FY 2014 did not have any opportunity to leave the military during that period, even if they wished to do so. However, they may be at high risk of separating when their term of service ends outside of our follow-up window. Thus, our study likely underestimates the total number of separations associated with sexual assaults and sexual harassment that survey results suggest occurred in FY 2014.

A second source of undercounting, and another study limitation, results from the fact that we assessed the effects of sexual assault and sexual harassment experiences that occurred only in FY 2014, yet some of the 98,000 members who separated in our follow-up window may have been influenced by sexual assault or sexual harassment experiences that happened before or after FY 2014. Thus, our estimates represent only a fraction of all of the sexual assault and sexual harassment experiences during the careers of the service members in our cohort.

Third, survey estimates of the prevalence of sexual assault and sexual harassment in the military typically report past-year prevalence rates among the service members who remain in the military by the end of that year (e.g., Hay and Elig, 1999; Breslin et al., 2019). Failure to survey individuals who separated during the year removes a possible high-risk group from the survey sample and may result in an undercount of both the past-year prevalence of sexual assault and the total number of individuals assaulted. To address this potential undercount, prevalence surveys could sample all members who served during the past year (i.e., not just those who remained in the force by the end of the year), or analytic adjustments to the prevalence estimates could be made based on reasonable assumptions about the sexual assault and sexual harassment exposures of members who served in the past year but separated by the time the survey was fielded. Currently, the WGRA screens out respondents who separated from the military between the time the survey's sample is drawn and the time the respondent receives the survey request. A low-cost approach to better estimating the prevalence of sexual assault among those who separated would be to allow those respondents to participate in the survey and then use their responses to estimate sexual assault prevalence among others who separated.

Sexual Assault and Harassment May Not Directly Cause Separation

Our finding that a large number of separations were uniquely associated with prior sexual assault and sexual harassment experiences does not prove that these experiences were the direct cause of these separations. We have shown only that prior sexual assault or sexual harassment helped to explain separations over and above what a large number of other factors could explain. We know, for instance, that members are more likely to separate when they reach the end of their current term of service, that enlisted members separate at higher rates than officers do, and that separations are associated with most of the other factors that we included in our model of the likelihood that each member would separate over the 28-month period. Our finding that knowledge of members' sexual assault or sexual harassment experiences predicted separations above and beyond all of these factors is consistent with the possibility that members separate at higher rates as a direct result of these experiences. However, it could also be that some other third factor accounts for both elevated separations and increased sexual harassment or sexual assault.

To illustrate how these associations may not reflect direct causation, consider a notional subgroup of service members who may face a wide range of unpleasant experiences in the military. This particular subgroup may have a high risk of sexual assault. It may be, however, that they also have higher rates of many other unpleasant experiences, all of which contribute to an elevated risk of separation. If this were the case, it may not be correct to say that the assaults per se elevated these members' risks. There may be many factors contributing to an increased risk of separation for this group. Therefore, throughout this report, when we identify elevated risks of separation, we describe them as being *associated* with sexual assault or sexual harassment experiences rather than directly *caused* by those experiences.

Recommendations

Our results suggest several avenues that DoD can pursue to better consider, understand, and address the effects of sexual assault and sexual harassment on service member separation.

Prioritize Prevention and Response to Sexual Harassment

DoD has invested considerable time and resources to improve prevention, reporting, and response systems for sexual assault (e.g., Sexual Assault Prevention and Response Office, undated). Sexual harassment has received comparatively less attention in recent years (GAO, 2017). The results of the present study suggest, however, that sexual harassment may impose appreciable costs to the military services and to service members that are substantially greater than those associated with sexual assault. Specifically, sexual harassment is associated with four times as many military separations as sexual assault is. With an estimated minimum of 8,000 members separating for reasons associated with sexual harassment, this study and previous research suggest that sexual harassment should be considered a significant infraction with damaging consequences for the military and military careers, as well as for the targets of the harassment (see, for example, Sims, Drasgow, and Fitzgerald, 2005; Willness, Steel, and Lee, 2007).

To promote prevention of and response to sexual harassment, DoD should elevate efforts that address these more-common workplace behaviors. We see several possible options that may improve prevention and response efforts, including incorporating additional information on sexual harassment into training and materials on sexual assault; promoting assessment, analysis, and reporting of factors associated with sexual harassment; creating more and new channels for reporting sexual harassment, particularly channels in which reporters can remain anonymous; tracking reports of sexual harassment by individual service members so that patterns of harassing behavior can be detected even across unit assignments; and increasing leadership accountability for actively addressing and reducing sexual harassment.

Ensure That Training and Prevention Materials Highlight That Men and Women Are Victims

Many of the sexual assault and sexual harassment prevention materials used across the services describe the features of these offenses in carefully gender-neutral terms. This is reasonable and understandable: Anyone could be a victim of sexual assault or sexual harassment, so it would be wrong to suggest a gender for either the target or the perpetrator. Nevertheless, without examples of the types of assault or harassment that men and women may encounter, there is a risk that recipients of these prevention materials will assume that these offenses specifically target women. As shown in this analysis, however, more men than women may be leaving the service prematurely for reasons associated with sexual assault or sexual harassment. To ensure that all forms of such offenses are prevented, therefore, we recommend highlighting the prevalence and forms of sexual assault and sexual harassment typically encountered by men and those encountered by women.

Continue Investigating How Sexual Assault Reporting Affects Separation Risk

Reporting sexual assaults ensures that service members can access the services and response systems that are available to them. If accessing these services reassures members who file a report that the military is determined to prosecute these crimes and provide care to victims, we might expect that those who file a report are less likely to decide that they cannot make a career in the military, compared with those who were sexually assaulted but do not file a report. On the other hand, if filing a report has negative repercussions for service members, such as exposing them to reprisals, ostracism, or maltreatment, then filing a report could actually increase separation risk.[3]

We investigated how reporting sexual assaults (versus not reporting them) affected separation rates and found no credible evidence that reporting is associated with either a decrease or an increase in separation risk among those who were sexually assaulted. However, this negative finding may be attributable to the fact that the sample size for these analyses was too small to produce reasonably precise estimates. This limitation could likely be overcome by combining data from several WGRA surveys. Doing so could provide DoD with valuable feedback on whether reporting is helping those who were sexually assaulted remain in the military.

Conclusion

The analyses described in this report provide an initial assessment of personnel separations associated with sexual assault and sexual harassment. However, this research is not without limitations. Our primary outcome variable was military separation within the 28 months after the sample frame was drawn. Analyses that consider a more extended time frame may provide additional insights into the associations between sexual assault and separation and between sexual harassment and separation. Furthermore, separation is not the only possible outcome of sexual assault and sexual harassment. As noted in Chapter One, multiple negative health and workplace outcomes are associated with these experiences, and our analyses did not address these outcomes. Additional assessments of data collected through DoD's biennial sexual assault and sexual harassment surveys may consider these health and workplace outcomes and the extent to which they mediate the association between victim experiences and separation. That said, our results highlight negative outcomes of sexual harassment and sexual assault for both service members and the military.

---

[3] This does not suggest what actions a service member should take. Rather, this suggests that filing a report might have positive or negative effects.

Separations by Service, Pay Grade Category, and Gender

Table A.1 shows the number of service members in the study cohort—by service, pay grade category, and gender—who separated from the military (for any reason) during the 28-month observation period. It also displays the percentage of cohort members who remained.

Table A.1
Service Member Separations from the Military During the 28-Month Observation Period, by Service, Pay Grade Category, and Gender

Service and Pay Grade Category	Gender	Remained in the Military After 28 Months	Left the Military After 28 Months	Percentage Remaining
Army				
Officers	Men	68,505	12,329	85
	Women	13,695	2,168	86
Enlisted	Men	275,127	77,677	78
	Women	40,564	13,018	76
Air Force				
Officers	Men	44,051	6,424	87
	Women	11,041	1,394	89
Enlisted	Men	175,900	29,083	86
	Women	39,938	6,951	85
Marine Corps				
Officers	Men	17,469	2,273	88
	Women	1,272	124	91
Enlisted	Men	130,418	22,574	85
	Women	10,254	2,126	83
Navy				
Officers	Men	39,080	4,804	89
	Women	8,008	793	91
Enlisted	Men	185,259	29,097	86
	Women	39,570	6,575	86

Discharge Codes Indicating a Failure to Adhere to Standards or Expectations

Our analysis of the reasons for discharge among separating service members examined those who received discharges for *failure to adhere to standards or expectations* (our label) versus those who had a discharge code indicating a voluntary separation, death, disability, or separation for unrecorded reasons. Table B.1 lists all discharge codes applied to study cohort members who were discharged during the 28-month observation period. Separation codes that we counted as failure to adhere to standards or expectations are indicated with a 1 in the last column of the table and a 0 otherwise. Note that the total number of separation codes identified is larger than the number of service members we treated as having separated from the military. This is because several of the codes listed in this table refer to transitions between different statuses in the military, such as immediately re-enlisting, entering Officer Candidate School, or entering a military academy. None of these transitions counted as separating from the military under our definitions.

Table B.1
Discharge Codes and Number of Service Members Separating During the 28-Month Observation Period

Interservice Separation Code	Description	Number of Separations	Failure to Adhere to Standards or Expectations
1067	Drugs	10,750	1
1084	Commission of a serious offense	9,202	1
1016	Unqualified for active duty, other	8,795	1
1017	Failure to meet weight or body fat standards	7,638	1
1086	Unsatisfactory performance (former Expeditious Discharge Program)	5,667	1
1065	Discreditable incidents, civilian or military	4,866	1
1085	Failure to meet minimum qualifications for retention	4,125	1
1002	Early release, insufficient retainability	3,730	1
1083	Pattern of minor disciplinary infractions	1,842	1
2009	Involuntary release, other	1,765	1
1064	Alcoholism	1,630	1
1078	Good of the service (discharge in lieu of court-martial)	1,329	1
2081	Unfitness or unacceptable conduct, other	1,028	1
1060	Character or behavior disorder	898	1
1073	Court-martial	727	1
1087	Entry level performance and conduct (former Trainee Discharge Program)	600	1
1071	Civil court conviction	387	1
1080	Misconduct, reason unknown	309	1
1102	Dropped from strength, imprisonment	308	1
1074	Fraudulent entry	240	1
1075	AWOL [away without leave] or desertion	151	1
2061	Motivational problems (apathy)	137	1
1101	Dropped from strength, desertion	134	1
1077	Sexual perversion	88	1
2017	Failure to meet weight or body fat standards	59	1
2084	Commission of a serious offense	49	1

Table B.1—Continued

Interservice Separation Code	Description	Number of Separations	Failure to Adhere to Standards or Expectations
2073	Court-martial	33	1
2067	Drugs	24	1
2102	Dropped from strength, imprisonment	24	1
2060	Character or behavior disorder	13	1
2016	Unqualified for active duty, other	10	1
1098	Breach of contract	9	1
2071	Civil court conviction	8	1
2101	Dropped from strength, desertion	8	1
2077	Sexual perversion	5	1
2064	Alcoholism	4	1
2065	Discreditable incidents, civilian or military	2	1
1072	Security	1	1
2072	Security	1	1
2085	Failure to meet minimum retention requirements	1	1
1000	Unknown or not applicable	200,586	0
1100	Immediate re-enlistment	171,879	0
1001	Expiration of term of service	151,096	0
1050	Retirement, 20 to 30 years of service	42,005	0
1012	Permanent disability retirement	19,364	0
1008	Early release, other, including RIF [reduction in force], VSI [voluntary separation incentive], and SSB [special separation bonus]	18,790	0
1011	Disability, severance pay	18,070	0
2050	Retirement, 20 to 30 years of service	17,793	0
1013	Temporary disability retirement	15,105	0
2001	Expiration of term of service	13,782	0
2000	Unknown or not applicable	7,998	0
1005	Early release, in the national interest	6,818	0
1051	Retirement, over 30 years of service	5,636	0
1052	Retirement, other	5,562	0

Table B.1—Continued

Interservice Separation Code	Description	Number of Separations	Failure to Adhere to Standards or Expectations
2005	Voluntary release, other, including VSI and SSB	4,588	0
1003	Early release, to attend school	3,945	0
2052	Retirement, other	3,177	0
1097	Parenthood	2,779	0
1099	Other	2,209	0
2079	Failure of selection for promotion	2,188	0
1094	Pregnancy	2,135	0
2051	Retirement, over 30 years of service	1,891	0
2012	Permanent disability retirement	1,788	0
2053	Retirement, failure of selection for promotion	1,585	0
2013	Temporary disability retirement	1,131	0
1032	Death, non-battle, other	969	0
1040	Officer commissioning program	896	0
1022	Dependency or hardship	643	0
1042	Military service academy	497	0
2011	Disability, severance pay	423	0
1010	Condition existing prior to service	416	0
1033	Death, cause not specified	260	0
1091	Erroneous enlistment or induction	257	0
2032	Death, non-battle, other	105	0
2033	Death, cause not specified	90	0
1031	Death, non-battle, disease	79	0
1090	Secretarial authority	50	0
2063	Failure of course of instruction	45	0
1014	Disability, no condition existing prior to service, no severance pay	43	0
1096	Conscientious objector	42	0
2094	Pregnancy	36	0
2002	Voluntary release, to attend school or to teach	35	0

Table B.1—Continued

Interservice Separation Code	Description	Number of Separations	Failure to Adhere to Standards or Expectations
1030	Death, battle casualty	33	0
2031	Death, non-battle, disease	23	0
2010	Condition existing prior to service	21	0
2022	Dependency or hardship	10	0
2090	Secretarial authority	7	0
2096	Conscientious objector	7	0
2030	Death, battle casualty	3	0
1092	Sole surviving family member	2	0
2099	Other	2	0
2003	Voluntary release, in the national interest	1	0
2007	Involuntary release, maximum age or service	1	0
2008	Involuntary release, convenience of the government	1	0
2014	Unknown	1	0
2092	Sole surviving family member	1	0
2103	Record correction	1	0

SOURCE: Defense Manpower Data Center, "Active Duty Military Personnel Master File," Excel spreadsheet, undated, provided to RAND May 2014 to August 2016.

NOTE: The interservice separation code refers to the last recorded separation code found in monthly DMDC personnel records for May 2014 to August 2016. The 1000-series codes are recorded for enlisted service members, and the 2000-series codes are for officers.

References

Bozdogan, Hamparsum, "Model Selection and Akaike's Information Criterion (AIC): The General Theory and Its Analytical Extensions," *Psychometrika*, 52(3), 1987, pp. 345–370.

Breslin, Rachel A., Lisa Davis, Kimberly Hylton, Ariel Hill, William Klauberg, Mark Petusky, and Ashlea Klahr, *2018 Workplace and Gender Relations Survey of Active Duty Members: Overview Report*, Alexandria, Va.: Office of People Analytics, Report No. 2019-027, May 2019.

Defense Manpower Data Center, "Active Duty Military Personnel Master File," Excel spreadsheet, undated, provided to RAND May 2014 to August 2016.

Dichter, Melissa E., and Gala True, "'This Is the Story of Why My Military Career Ended Before It Should Have': Premature Separation from Military Service Among U.S. Women Veterans," *Affilia: Journal of Women and Social Work*, Vol. 30, No. 2, 2015, pp. 187–199.

Farris, Coreen, Lisa H. Jaycox, Terry L. Schell, Amy E. Street, Dean G. Kilpatrick, and Terri Tanielian, "Sexual Harassment and Gender Discrimination Findings: Active Component," in Andrew R. Morral, Kristie L. Gore, and Terry L. Schell, eds., *Sexual Assault and Sexual Harassment in the U.S. Military: Volume 2. Estimates for Department of Defense Service Members from the 2014 RAND Military Workplace Study*, Santa Monica, Calif.: RAND Corporation, RR-870/2-1-OSD, 2015, pp. 31–54. As of January 24, 2021:
https://www.rand.org/pubs/research_reports/RR870z2-1.html

Farris, Coreen, Amy Street, Andrew R. Morral, Lisa Jaycox, and Dean Kilpatrick, "Measurement of Sexual Harassment and Sexual Assault," in Andrew R. Morral, Kristie L. Gore, and Terry L. Schell, eds., *Sexual Assault and Sexual Harassment in the U.S. Military: Volume 1. Design of the 2014 RAND Military Workplace Study*, Santa Monica, Calif.: RAND Corporation, RR-870/1-OSD, 2014, pp. 7–25. As of January 24, 2021:
https://www.rand.org/pubs/research_reports/RR870z1.html

Fitzgerald, Louise F., Fritz Drasgow, and Vicki J. Magley, "Sexual Harassment in the Armed Forces: A Test of An Integrated Model," *Military Psychology*, Vol. 11, No. 3, 1999, pp. 329–343.

Fitzgerald, Louise F., Vicki J. Magley, Fritz Drasgow, and Craig R. Waldo, "Measuring Sexual Harassment in the Military: The Sexual Experiences Questionnaire (SEQ-DoD)," *Military Psychology*, Vol. 11, No. 3, 1999, pp. 243–263.

Fitzgerald, Louise F., Suzanne Swan, and Karla Fischer, "Why Didn't She Just Report Him? The Psychological and Legal Implications of Women's Reponses to Sexual Harassment," *Journal of Social Issues*, Vol. 51, No. 1, 1995, pp. 117–138.

Frayne, Susan M., Katherine M. Skinner, Lisa M. Sullivan, Tara J. Tripp, Cheryl S. Hankin, Nancy R. Kressin, and Donald R. Miller, "Medical Profile of Women Veterans Administration Outpatients Who Report a History of Sexual Assault Occurring While in the Military," *Journal of Women's Health and Gender-Based Medicine*, Vol. 8, No. 6, 1999, pp. 835–845.

Friedman, Jerome H., "Greedy Function Approximation: A Gradient Boosting Machine," *Annals of Statistics*, Vol. 29, No. 5, 2001, pp. 1189–1232.

GAO—*See* U.S. Government Accountability Office.

Ghosh-Dastidar, Bonnie, Terry L. Schell, Andrew R. Morral, and Marc N. Elliot, "The Efficacy of Sampling Weights for Correcting Nonresponse Bias," in Andrew R. Morral, Kristie L. Gore, and Terry L. Schell, eds., *Sexual Assault and Sexual Harassment in the U.S. Military: Volume 4. Investigations of Potential Bias in Estimates from the 2014 RAND Military Workplace Study*, Santa Monica, Calif.: RAND Corporation, RR-870/6-OSD, 2016, pp. 21–70. As of September 21, 2020: https://www.rand.org/pubs/research_reports/RR870z6.html

Goldberg, Matthew S., *A Survey of Enlisted Retention: Models and Findings*, Alexandria, Va.: CNA Corporation, November 2001.

Harned, Melanie S., Alayne J. Ormerod, Patrick A. Palmieri, Linda L. Collinsworth, and Maggie Reed, "Sexual Assault and Other Types of Sexual Harassment by Workplace Personnel: A Comparison of Antecedents and Consequences," *Journal of Occupational Health Psychology*, Vol. 7, No. 2, 2002, pp. 174–188.

Hay, Mary Sue, and Timothy W. Elig, "The 1995 Department of Defense Sexual Harassment Survey: Overview and Methodology," *Military Psychology*, Vol. 11, No. 3, 1999, pp. 233–242.

Jaycox, Lisa H., Terry L. Schell, Andrew R. Morral, Amy Street, Coreen Farris, Dean Kilpatrick, and Terri Tanielian, "Sexual Assault Findings: Active Component," in Andrew R. Morral, Kristie L. Gore, and Terry L. Schell, eds., *Sexual Assault and Sexual Harassment in the U.S. Military: Volume 2. Estimates for Department of Defense Service Members from the 2014 RAND Military Workplace Study*, Santa Monica, Calif.: RAND Corporation, RR-870/2-1-OSD, 2015, pp. 9–30. As of January 24, 2021: https://www.rand.org/pubs/research_reports/RR870z2-1.html

Katz, Lori S., Cristi Huffman, and Geta Cojucar, "In Her Own Words: Semi-Structured Interviews of Women Veterans Who Experienced Military Sexual Assault," *Journal of Contemporary Psychotherapy*, Vol. 47, No. 3, 2017, pp. 181–189.

Kimerling, Rachel, Amy E. Street, Joanne Pavao, Mark W. Smith, Ruth C. Cronkite, Tyson H. Holmes, and Susan M. Frayne, "Military-Related Sexual Trauma Among Veterans Health Administration Patients Returning from Afghanistan and Iraq," *American Journal of Public Health*, Vol. 100, No. 8, 2010, pp. 1409–1412.

Martin, Lee, Leora N. Rosen, Doris B. Durand, Kathryn H. Knudson, and Robert H. Stretch, "Psychological and Physical Health Effects of Sexual Assaults and Nonsexual Traumas Among Male and Female United States Army Soldiers," *Behavioral Medicine*, Vol. 26, No. 1, 2000, pp. 23–33.

Mattock, Michael G., Beth J. Asch, James Hosek, Christopher Whaley, and Christina Panis, *Toward Improved Management of Officer Retention: A New Capability for Assessing Policy Options*, Santa Monica, Calif.: RAND Corporation, RR-764-OSD, 2014. As of January 24, 2021: https://www.rand.org/pubs/research_reports/RR764.html

McCaffrey, Daniel F., Greg Ridgeway, and Andrew R. Morral, "Propensity Score Estimation with Boosted Regression for Evaluating Causal Effects in Observational Studies," *Psychological Methods*, Vol. 9, No. 4, 2004, pp. 403–425.

Military Compensation and Retirement Modernization Commission, *Report of the Military Compensation and Retirement Modernization Commission: Final Report*, Washington, D.C., January 2015.

Millegan, Jeffrey, Emma K. Milburn, Cynthia A. LeardMann, Amy E. Street, Diane Williams, Daniel W. Trone, and Nancy F. Crum Cianflone, "Recent Sexual Trauma and Adverse Health and Occupational Outcomes Among U.S. Service Women," *Journal of Traumatic Stress*, Vol. 28, No. 4, 2015, pp. 298–306.

Millegan, Jeffrey, Lawrence Wang, Cynthia A. LeardMann, Derek Miletich, and Amy E. Street, "Sexual Trauma and Adverse Health and Occupational Outcomes Among Men Serving in the U.S. Military," *Journal of Traumatic Stress*, Vol. 29, No. 2, 2016, pp. 132–140.

Morral, Andrew R., Kristie L. Gore, and Terry L. Schell, eds., *Sexual Assault and Sexual Harassment in the U.S. Military: Volume 1. Design of the 2014 RAND Military Workplace Study*, Santa Monica, Calif.: RAND Corporation, RR-870/1-OSD, 2014. As of January 24, 2021:
https://www.rand.org/pubs/research_reports/RR870z1.html

———, eds., *Sexual Assault and Sexual Harassment in the U.S. Military: Volume 2. Estimates for Department of Defense Service Members from the 2014 RAND Military Workplace Study*, Santa Monica, Calif.: RAND Corporation, RR-870/2-1-OSD, 2015a. As of January 24, 2021:
https://www.rand.org/pubs/research_reports/RR870z2-1.html

———, eds., *Sexual Assault and Sexual Harassment in the U.S. Military: Volume 3. Estimates for Coast Guard Service Members from the 2014 RAND Military Workplace Study*, Santa Monica, Calif.: RAND Corporation, RR-870/4-USCG, 2015b. As of January 24, 2021:
https://www.rand.org/pubs/research_reports/RR870z4.html

———, eds., *Sexual Assault and Sexual Harassment in the U.S. Military: Volume 4. Investigations of Potential Bias in Estimates from the 2014 RAND Military Workplace Study*, Santa Monica, Calif.: RAND Corporation, RR-870/6-OSD, 2016. As of January 24, 2021:
https://www.rand.org/pubs/research_reports/RR870z6.html

Murdoch, Maureen, Melissa A. Polusny, James Hodges, and Diane Cowper, "The Association Between In-Service Sexual Harassment and Post-Traumatic Stress Disorder Among Department of Veterans Affairs Disability Applicants," *Military Medicine*, Vol. 171, No. 2, 2006, pp. 166–173.

Murdoch, Maureen, John Barron Pryor, Melissa Anderson Polusny, and Gary Dean Gackstetter, "Functioning and Psychiatric Symptoms Among Military Men and Women Exposed to Sexual Stressors," *Military Medicine*, Vol. 172, No. 7, 2007, pp. 718–725.

Public Law 88-352, Civil Rights Act of 1964, July 2, 1964.

Ridgeway, Greg, *Generalized Boosted Models: A Guide to the Gbm Package*, September 14, 2018. As of December 3, 2019:
http://healthstat.snu.ac.kr/CRAN/web/packages/gbm/vignettes/gbm.pdf

Rosellini, Anthony J., Amy E. Street, Robert J. Ursano, Wai Tat Chiu, Steven G. Heeringa, John Monahan, James A. Naifeh, Maria V. Petukhova, Ben Y. Reis, Nancy A. Sampson, Paul D. Bliese, Murray B. Stein, Alan M. Zaslavsky, and Ronald C. Kessler, "Sexual Assault Victimization and Mental Health Treatment, Suicide Attempts, and Career Outcomes Among Women in the U.S. Army," *American Journal of Public Health*, Vol. 107, No. 5, 2017, pp. 732–739.

Rust, Keith F., and J. N. K. Rao, "Variance Estimation for Complex Surveys Using Replication Techniques," *Statistical Methods in Medical Research*, Vol. 5, No. 3, 1996, pp. 283–310.

Ryan, Margaret A. K., Tyler C. Smith, Besa Smith, Paul Amoroso, Edward J. Boyko, Gregory C. Gray, Gary D. Gackstetter, James R. Riddle, Timothy S. Wells, Gia Gumbs, Thomas E. Corbeil, and Tomoko I. Hooper, "Millennium Cohort: Enrollment Begins a 21-Year Contribution to Understanding the Impact of Military Service," *Journal of Clinical Epidemiology*, Vol. 60, No. 2, 2007, pp. 181–191.

Sadler, Anne G., Brenda M. Booth, Michelle A. Mengeling, and Bradley N. Doebbeling, "Life Span and Repeated Violence Against Women During Military Service: Effects on Health Status and Outpatient Utilization," *Journal of Women's Health*, Vol. 13, No. 7, 2004, pp. 799–811.

Sagawa, Shirley, and Nancy Duff Campbell, *Sexual Harassment of Women in the Military*, Washington, D.C.: National Women's Law Center, 1992.

Schneider, Kimberly T., Suzanne Swan, and Louise F. Fitzgerald, "Job-Related and Psychological Effects of Sexual Harassment in the Workplace: Empirical Evidence from Two Organizations," *Journal of Applied Psychology*, Vol. 82, No. 3, 1997, pp. 401–415.

Sexual Assault Prevention and Response Office, "SAPRO Overview," fact sheet, Washington, D.C., undated. As of January 4, 2021:
http://sapr.mil/public/docs/press/SAPROOverviewSlickSheet_20160725.pdf

Sims, Carra S., Fritz Drasgow, and Louise F. Fitzgerald, "The Effects of Sexual Harassment on Turnover in the Military: Time-Dependent Modeling," *Journal of Applied Psychology*, Vol. 90, No. 6, 2005, pp. 1141–1152.

Smith, Brian N., Jillian C. Shipherd, Jennifer L. Schuster, Dawne S. Vogt, Lynda A. King, and Daniel W. King, "Posttraumatic Stress Symptomatology as a Mediator of the Association Between Military Sexual Trauma and Post-Deployment Physical Health in Women," *Journal of Trauma & Dissociation*, Vol. 12, No. 3, 2011, pp. 275–289.

Smith, Tyler C., Deborah L. Wingard, Margaret A. K. Ryan, Donna Kritz-Silverstein, Donald J. Slymen, and James F. Sallis, "Prior Assault and Posttraumatic Stress Disorder After Combat Deployment," *Epidemiology*, Vol. 19, No. 3, 2008, pp. 505–512.

Street, Amy E., Jaimie L. Gradus, Jane Stafford, and Kacie Kelly, "Gender Differences in Experiences of Sexual Harassment: Data from a Male-Dominated Environment," *Journal of Consulting and Clinical Psychology*, Vol. 75, No. 3, 2007, pp. 464–474.

Street, Amy E., Jane Stafford, Clare M. Mahan, and Ann Hendricks, "Sexual Harassment and Assault Experienced by Reservists During Military Service: Prevalence and Health Correlates," *Journal of Rehabilitation Research and Development*, Vol. 45, No. 3, 2008, pp. 409–419.

Suris, Alina, and Lisa Lind, "Military Sexual Trauma: A Review of Prevalence and Associated Health Consequences in Veterans," *Trauma, Violence, & Abuse*, Vol. 9, No. 4, 2008, pp. 250–269.

Turchik, Jessica A., and Susan M. Wilson, "Sexual Assault in the U.S. Military: A Review of the Literature and Recommendations for the Future," *Aggression and Violent Behavior*, Vol. 15, No. 4, 2010, pp. 267–277.

U.S. Government Accountability Office, *Military Personnel: Personnel and Cost Data Associated with Implementing DOD's Homosexual Conduct Policy*, Washington, D.C., GAO-11-170, January 2011.

———, *Sexual Violence: Actions Needed to Improve DoD's Efforts to Address the Continuum of Unwanted Sexual Behaviors*, Washington, D.C., GAO-18-33, December 2017.

Willness, Chelsea R., Piers Steel, and Kibeom Lee, "A Meta-Analysis of the Antecedents and Consequences of Workplace Sexual Harassment," *Personnel Psychology*, Vol. 60, No. 1, 2007, pp. 127–162.